AF680291

© 2024 Efrat Ron

All rights reserved. No portion of this book may
be reproduced in any form without permission from the publisher,
except as permitted by U.S. copyright law.

Library of Congress registration number: TX 9-372-123

ISBN 9798875986567

9798234203823

9798234203820

For rights and permissions, please contact:

Efrat Ron

Witchwerevamp1313@gmail.com

Contents

Disclaimer

This book is not intended for treating or diagnosing any condition. It is a rendition of my daily practices for living with PTSD. It is advisable to seek professional medical attention for any symptoms you are experiencing. Medical attention can include consulting a licensed therapist specializing in trauma work, alongside a physician trained in mental health issues, and exploring various treatment protocols. These may or may not bring back repressed memories. Seek medical attention if you feel unsafe, have thoughts of harming yourself or others, or feel unwell.

Disclaimer

This book is not intended for treating or diagnosing any condition. It is a rendition of my daily practices for living with PTSD. It is advisable to seek professional medical attention for any symptoms you are experiencing. Medical attention can include considering a licensed therapist specializing in trauma work alongside a physician trained in mental health issues, and exploring various treatment protocols. These may or may not bring back repressed memories. Seek medical attention if you feel unsafe, have thoughts of harming yourself or others, or feel unwell.

Acknowledgements

To the therapists who helped me get to where I am in life, thank you.

To the editors who helped me ensure that my words made sense to the world, thank you.

Dedication

To my grandmother Tina, the strongest woman
I have ever met in my entire life.

Tina spent time teaching me about life in her own way; she taught me to cook, bake, sew, and knit. She was a survivor who escaped from the concentration camps in Europe during World War II.

To my friends John V. Leggat Sr. and Shaun Ferguson,
who had open hearts, open ears, and an understanding
that bad stuff happens in life.

Introduction

Enclosed are some ways I live my life, and I have PTSD, or Post-Traumatic Stress Disorder, resulting from experiences of rape, assault, mental abuse, stalkers, and bullying, to name just a few. Living life with PTSD is a challenge, not to mention accomplishing anything else.

Additionally, many people are misdiagnosed with severe depression when they actually have PTSD.

PTSD and depression, including severe depression, have many similar symptoms and often overlap in ways that can include:

- Avoiding people, places, or things
- Sleeping a lot or very little
- Feeling nervous
- Experiencing anxiety
- Living in fear
- Being afraid
- Avoiding communication with others

However, the biggest difference between PTSD and depression is:

With PTSD, you relive the memory of the trauma or the events causing the trauma repeatedly, while with depression, you DO NOT.

This experience changed my life when my therapist, Dr. Brown explained it to me. It was a significant breakthrough for me, as I had repressed my traumatic memories so deeply that I couldn't recall them, and when I did catch a glimpse, it was like the constant static on old TV stations. To this day, I am so grateful to Dr. Brown for diagnosing me with PTSD, not depression. This diagnosis paved the way for the treatments I tried, which at least allowed me some good nights' sleep and relief.

It also opened the door for me to let people back into my life, to feel and express emotions, and to find that special someone (though I wasn't looking, he'll tell you he found me, and then we got separated). It gave me the freedom to discuss with my physicians the medications or drug therapies they prescribed and whether they contributed to my overall therapy goals.

After I stopped seeing Dr. Brown, I moved to a different state due to her nearing retirement, I began seeking therapists specializing in trauma, knowledgeable or trained in various aspects of trauma work, and focused on healing myself. The journey has been long and challenging, but along the way, I learned to fully love myself, including all the damage I've endured, and to shift my mindset towards a more positive life perspective. This doesn't mean I ignore life's dark or negative aspects; rather, I embrace these aspects of myself instead of trying to eliminate them. I love both the positive and negative sides of myself equally because they make me who I am.

I sought different types of therapy, including individual therapists and group sessions, to acquire new skills that *might* help me achieve my goals: better sleep most of the week and finding friendships or relationships. I also adopted a parakeet and later got another, caring for them until they both passed away at nearly 9 years old. The skills I learned laid the foundation for me to persist through various types of therapy until I had tried all the conventional methods. Now, only experimental therapies remain for me. But don't feel bad for me. It shows the amount of persistence I have to heal, grow as a person, and find ideas to assist me in my journey with PTSD.

There are absolutely no rules or paths set in stone, and this book should serve as a guideline for finding your path. You are the only one in control of your life. You can apply any therapy and piece of advice in any way you choose, as long as you do not harm yourself or others. It might not work for you. It could be the best thing you ever do for yourself. You won't know until you try for yourself and see what happens. However, learning the therapies and skills, adjusting your mindset, adapting them to your life, and understanding that they may not work for everyone takes time. That's fine; if something doesn't work, find something else. Again, it's YOUR life.

But you won't know until you try them, work with them in your own way, and invest time and money in therapy.

In other words, this book is only a guideline, based on my many years of therapy.

After many years of trying to make life work.

Basically, do what you want – it's your life to live.

But my suggestion is to read the book, attend therapy, and relearn how to live life.

Because life will throw curveballs at you, you might as well learn how to catch them or avoid being hit by them.

What do you really have to lose?

MEMORIES

Memories can be either good or bad. Personally, I prefer the good ones that make me feel warm and cozy, as opposed to those that wake me up screaming.

PTSD is, in essence, the constant remembering of bad memories or a specific point in time, over and over again, without changing the ending.

It can always be there, waking you up at the same time every night, or it can appear unexpectedly, triggered by a smell or someone's resemblance.

However, you can do something about it.

Essentially, you have a CHOICE in how you want to live your life.

The question is do you?

Do you let your PTSD take the reins?

Do you let your fear control you?

Do you try different therapies until one works most of the time?

Do you experiment with various skills or techniques to make your life livable and start to thrive?

Let me tell you a bit about myself. You already know I have PTSD, but let me say that I have tried almost everything under the sun.

I have tried medications because the doctors thought I had severe depression and I've tried many medications in different combinations (my long drug allergy list is proof of that; I give doctors drug classes because who has time during an office visit to list every single one). Basically, nothing the doctors prescribed provided relief or even a few nights of good sleep. Now, I have a huge list of medications I cannot take, so I needed another method to live my life.

I tried DBT (Dialectical Behavioral Therapy) and CBT (Cognitive Behavioral Therapy), and they worked and continue to work to some extent. These therapies essentially provide tools to change how you think and perceive the world after experiencing trauma. To this day, I still use some of the tools taught in those therapy sessions because they have become so ingrained in me that I use them without thinking. The skills are adaptable to what's happening in my life and are not a rigid structure.

As a sidebar, I only list some of the books I used and how they applied to me while I was seeing a specially trained therapist during both private and group therapy. Each therapist has a list of books they have either read, know of, or recommend reading to assist, so ask your therapist and get some books. Also, some libraries have these books available for checkout, so you should be able to get a copy from somewhere. So go and get therapy, whether individual or group, whatever you can afford, or your insurance allows. Therapy has been a lifesaver for me and has immensely assisted me in my journey.

I also did some work using light and sensory therapy with a technique called EMDR (Eye Movement Desensitization and Reprocessing). This technique is a significant intervention but comes with a forewarning: it takes weeks or months to get through, you have to relive some trauma for it to work, and importantly, you need to be able to sleep for it to process effectively. That was my experience with it – a big problem for someone with PTSD. I highly recommend finding someone who can guide you through it as it is much easier. There are therapists specializing in this treatment, and sometimes it's covered by insurance, so if you think it's the right fit, go and get a consultation.

There are experimental treatments undergoing trials, but they are not covered by insurance companies. Some require significant sums of money and, crucially, sleep.

Let me quickly and briefly explain why sleep is vital for people recovering from PTSD. During the deepest part of sleep, your brain processes memories, categorizing them as good, bad, neutral, learning, etc. It begins to sort everything you experienced during the day, ideally reducing stress hormone levels to the starting point. With PTSD, there's like a switch that keeps bringing back the trauma, hoping it gets processed into some place in your brain. The problem is that the switch for that trauma is broken or stuck, so the memory isn't processed properly, if at all.

Even if a memory is partially processed, it can cause flashbacks and flares as the brain tries to process it. If you can't sleep throughout the night, the brain malfunctions in a way. EMDR, for instance, helps process the emotional part of the trauma while decreasing the body's response to the memory of the trauma. It reduces the emotional response to the memory or trigger, allowing you to deal with the actual memory or rationalize through the trauma without the emotions. This way, you don't get 'stuck' in the fear, anxiety, anger, or extreme panic associated with the memory of the trauma. But again, you need to be able to sleep through the night.

So, sleep is crucial in recovery, and if you cannot sleep through the night, things go haywire. The trauma cannot get processed, causing you harm just because of the lack of sleep.

Flaring Tempers

When your PTSD flares, you can scream, be mad, be angry, or you can ignore the memory. You have a choice: to ignore the memory, to scream at it, or to be mad at what happened.

And then what?

What if you ignored the memory, not by suppressing or repressing it, which involves pushing the memory deep down?

What if, instead of using your energy to scream or be mad, you:

Do something good for yourself.

Do something good for someone you know.

Give an authentic compliment to someone in line.

Compliment someone walking by.

Do something good for a random stranger.

Engage in more relaxing activities like drawing, knitting, dancing, singing, or playing an instrument—whatever moves you. How about taking a walk, run, bath, or doing whatever makes you feel warm and fuzzy?

Talk to a friend.

Do something nice.

Take a short nap (yes, really).

But remember, sometimes there is nothing better than a good scream in the car, a room alone, or wherever no one is listening to you. Basically, what I am saying is that it depends on the moment you are in. Sometimes, feeling that negative feeling is the only thing that helps you move forward. So, feel it and then move forward. Please make it a habit not to dwell on that negative moment for too long.

I recently relearned something in a new light. Dwelling on anger can be a good thing if you gain insight into it, are able to speak about it appropriately to others, or find a resolution for the problem. But here is the key: put a timer on it and then move forward. Do NOT let that anger continue for more than a specific time period.

Let's say you give the memory a day to make you angry. Then give it a day, or up to a whole day, and then move forward. Try, during that day, to pick your mood or do something constructive. Do not let that anger be the only feeling you experience that day. If there is no other feeling than being in a neutral mood, let that be the goal rather than being only angry that day.

Self-Love

vs Self Hatred

Stop worrying about what others think of you.
You must first love yourself.

(People mostly think about themselves anyway.)

Stop caring about whom others want you to befriend, love, or spend your precious time with.

It's your life, so spend it with the people YOU choose.

Spend your money on whom YOU wish, even if that includes you.

Prioritize yourself financially. Save for a rainy day, a big trip, or something you've always wanted but were hesitant to purchase.

Don't always depend on someone else to buy things for you.

Learn to be both independent and dependent.

Be selective about who you confide in. Friends who treat themselves well will also likely treat you well, so take care of yourself.

Again, it's your life. Live it as you wish (but don't harm others).

Be true to yourself as you will evolve over time; embrace that and love yourself, flaws included.

Learn to appreciate silence and solitude.

Learn to love every part of yourself.

Respect your body and its signals. Understanding your triggers helps with long-term emotional regulation. This awareness can guide you toward what brings happiness and what causes stress.

You are a beautiful human being.

Value yourself and your contributions.

Bad Feelings

Feel the bad feelings—it's okay; they will pass eventually, and a new feeling will take their place. This happens constantly throughout the day. Feelings and thoughts are fleeting and only last a long time if you allow them to fester.

Can you name the feelings you are having?

Name each feeling separately?

How does each feeling make you feel and act?

Do you remember when you were first told you were bad for having a certain memory?

Were you told to be quiet?

Spend some time with yourself; get to know yourself. Figure out what triggers you, and then find a way to deal with it. Remember, you cannot live in a bubble, and the world is terrifying.

Here's a quick story—I had wanted to be a mother until I realized I would not be able to handle a child's demands on me and deal with my PTSD. It also helped me realize that no man I met was willing to sacrifice their time and money for the child. I was somehow expected to provide for them all financially and emotionally. Additionally, my body stopped having periods, meaning I went into really early menopause and had severe symptoms associated with it.

The hot flashes and pools of sweat when I slept were not fun. The added anxiety I felt, becoming self-conscious due to the hot sweats, did not help with my PTSD or my sleep. So, I gave up on being a mother. It seems like an easy thing to do, but it was a difficult decision that I realized worked for me due to my particular situation. Something had to give, and that was being a mother; it simply was not in my cards. I accepted and grieved the loss of this life event because I could not become a mother.

So grieve. Give it time. Then move on.

LIFE

Life can be really bad sometimes.

Sometimes it lasts a long while, and sometimes it does not.

Life is good. Life is fun and exciting.

That is a fact.

Anyone telling you otherwise is a liar, delusional, and has their head up their ass to the point that they cannot see clearly. (Stay away from these types of people; they are toxic, in my opinion.)

Just learn to deal with it. Life gets better. Life gets bad.

Life is unfair. Life is cruel.

I live my life by the moments: some good, some bad, some are just moments.

Life can be really bad sometimes.

Sometimes it lasts a long while, and sometimes it does not.

Life is good. Life is fun and exciting.

That is a fact.

Anyone telling you otherwise is a liar, delusional, and has their head up their ass to the point that they cannot see clearly. (Stay away from these types of people; they are toxic, in my opinion.)

Just learn to deal with it. Life gets better; life gets bad.

Life is unfair. Life is cruel.

Take my life by the moments: some good, some bad, some are just moments.

TOXICITY

Eliminate toxic people from your life.

They might be family members with good intentions who, nonetheless, make your life miserable. They could also be your best friend who drains your energy.

Winning the lottery is akin to having a few good friends while distancing yourself from the rest. Seek out those who aim to uplift and assist you, those who genuinely listen because you are important to them, and value what you say—not for gossip.

Casual friends are acceptable, but don't allow them to occupy too much of your time or mental space.

Surround yourself with people who bring meaning to your life.

Cease posting on social media if it's toxic.

However, don't shun social media altogether, as it's a common platform for event announcements. Being social when possible is important.

Life is inherently full of contradictions.

Grateful

Find something for which to be grateful.

Anything.

Perhaps the weather is getting cooler. Maybe you just saw the greenest blade of grass, the fuzziest flower ever, or the softest-looking cloud. Perhaps you reached your destination in record time, with no major delays or encountering many red lights. Consider any small thing that made you smile, even just a little bit. You can be grateful for anything that makes you slightly happier.

Make it a habit to be grateful for one small, tiny thing each day.

Eventually, your gratitude will expand to more things, and you will begin to see the world through a different set of eyes.

However, it takes time.

Being grateful helps to get through the bad days.

CONTRADICTIONS

Life is contradictory.

Just get used to it.

Life is not black and white; it is actually all kinds of colors and many shades of those colors.

Figure out a way to deal with life and people being contradictory.

I am sorry life is not a bunch of great-smelling roses all the time.

But sometimes, life is good and full of surprises.

In my opinion, just enjoy life and all its contradictions.

Learn to see all the variations and colors in life.

THERAPY

Great therapists help, I swear.

I have had a few.

They have saved my life several times and probably don't even realize it.

I remember their lessons and the skills they taught me.

Even when we argued, they still saw something good in me—something worth saving.

The website https://www.psychologytoday.com/us is an excellent starting point for finding a therapist or doctor in your area. It will be the best investment you make in managing your PTSD, rebuilding, and taking back your life.

NO

I remember my therapists teaching me the most powerful and most hated word ever uttered in the English language:

"No."

This word creates boundaries that separate you from others, making your experiences unique.

Learning to use this word can be difficult, but it gives you back your choice in what you do with your life while creating a safe space and separating you from toxic people. When you start using this word, it will be awful, even more anxiety-inducing, but as you get used to respecting your boundaries, it will become easier.

Repeat this word if you need to make your point.

It's your life.

It's your body.

It's your mind.

It's your journey.

It's your CHOICE.

CONTROL

There is something I need to say about having control.

You are not responsible for the actions of other people, regardless of what you think or have been told.

YOU

ARE

NOT

RESPONSIBLE

FOR

THE

ACTIONS

OF

OTHER

PEOPLE.

Really.

Please let go of that control. It won't help you in any way, shape, or form; rather, it will cause you anxiety, anger, shame, guilt, and drive you mad. It will lead to the end of relationships and the rise of tensions.

Let's say it again, as it's worth repeating.

YOU

ARE

NOT

IN

CONTROL

OF

OTHER

PEOPLE'S

ACTIONS.

Focus on the goodness you can bring into your own life, your health, and the relationships that bring you moments of joy.

Focus on living each moment and what you can change for yourself. Focus on your dreams and the steps you can take to make those dreams come true.

Focus on yourself.

PERFECTION

You are not perfect, and you cannot become the perfect:

Wife

Husband

Brother

Sister

Friend

Coworker

Person

I know that with trauma, it can seem that if you behave a certain way, date or talk, live and work a certain way, or live in a certain place, the trauma won't happen again. It is one of those beliefs that if I do things a certain way, I won't get hurt or have to go through THAT experience again. Guess what?

It might... just... happen... again... and I am sorry.

There are unfortunately no guarantees in life, and this is one of those instances.

It's not because you were not perfect or because you are not loved, but because the world is scary and not perfect.

And then again, that trauma experience might NOT ever happen again, so who knows? Life is unpredictable, and that is what makes life interesting.

But you will, and other people in your life will, make mistakes, and that just means we are human and NOT PERFECT.

Not only that, trying to reach that unattainable goal of being perfect means you will become more tense, more stressed, more NOT LIKE YOU.

And I LIKE THE REAL YOU, the one that is not PERFECT, the one that makes MISTAKES, and tells me what is on their mind. I want to hang out with that person who knows how to say "I am sorry" and mean it but can also LAUGH at themselves.

That is the person I want to hang out with. The person who says, "I have all these feelings, and if you have time, let me share them with you."

The person who does not know those dance moves and still dances with me. Or the lyrics to the songs and still sings that song.

I want to hang out with that imperfect human who does not want to reach that unattainable goal and yet wants to spend time with me.

Who do you want to hang out with? The perfect person? Or the imperfect person?

You cannot make the trauma go away, but you can learn to live your life again.

You cannot make those memories disappear, I wish they could disappear. But those memories do not have to be the driving force or in the driver's seat of your life, unless you give them that power.

You cannot make the pains of loss go away, but you can learn to deal with them.

And that is what I think it is, learning to deal with the events that have happened and building a life that you enjoy. Because it is your life, you might as well enjoy it, and live your life your way.

ART

Living with PTSD is like embarking on a journey that is uniquely yours, and finding joy in this journey can be a beautiful process. These next two pages are dedicated to creating beauty and joy, a little oasis in your world. I've included pages for coloring and blank spaces for drawing or jotting down your thoughts. Think of them as a canvas for your emotions, a place to express yourself freely and creatively.

Remember, it's completely okay if coloring, drawing, or writing isn't your thing. There's no one-size-fits-all in the journey of healing and finding joy. Feel free to skip these pages. Your path to joy might be different, and that's absolutely fine. Perhaps you find joy in music, in walking through nature, or in simply sitting quietly. Embrace whatever brings you peace and happiness.

If you do choose to use these pages, grab whatever you have – a pencil, crayons, markers, paint, or even lipstick. Let your imagination run wild. There are no rules here. No need for perfection. Just the freedom to express whatever you feel, in whatever way feels right to you.

This moment marks a new chapter in your life with PTSD. It's the beginning of acknowledging your experiences, embracing your resilience, and learning to find moments of joy and beauty in your life. PTSD may be a part of your story, but it doesn't define you. You are capable of creating moments of happiness and peace in your life. May you find joy in the small things, strength in your journey, and comfort in knowing that you are not alone. Let this be the start of living your life with PTSD, not just surviving it, but finding enjoyment and fulfillment in it.

References

1. Psychology Today, www.psychologytoday.com
2. Bessel Van Der Kolf MD. *The Body Keeps The Score; Brain, Mind and Body in the Healing of Trauma.* Penquin Books. 2015
3. Marsha Linehan, *Cognitive-Behavioral Treatment of Borderline Personality Disorder 1st Edition*, The Guilford Press. 1993
4. Brene Brule PhD, MSW. *Daring Greatly, How the Courage to Being Vulnerable Transforms the Way We Live, Love, Parent, and Lead.* Penquin Random House. 2012.
5. Brene Brule PhD MSW. *The Gifts of Imperfection, Let Go of Who You Think You Are and Embrace Who You Are.* Hazelden Publishing. 2010.
6. Brene Brule PhD MSW. *Rising Strong, How The Ability to Reset Transforms The Way We Live, Love, Parent, and Lead.* Penquin Random House. 2015
7. Bryon Katie. *Question Your Thinking, Change the World.* Hay House. 2007.
8. Bryon Katie. *The Little book*. 2022
9. Charlotte Davis Kasl PhD. *Women, Sex, and Addiction, A Search for Love and Power*. Houghton Mifflin Harcourt Publishing Company. 1989.

10. Peter A Levine PhD. *Healing Trauma, A Program for Restoring The Wisdom of the Body*. Sounds True. 2008

11. Peter A Levine PhD, Fredrick Anne. *Awakening the Tiger; Healing Trauma*. 1997.

12. Pema Chodon. *The Places That Scare You, A Guide for Fearlessness in Difficult Times*. Shambhala Publications Inc. 2001.

13. Pia Mellody and Lawerencpe S Freundlich. *The Intimacy Factor, The Ground Rules for Overcoming the Obstacles to Truth, Respect, and Everlasting Love*. Harper Collins. 2007.

14. Ming-Dao, Deng. *365 Tao, Daily Meditations*. HarperOne. 1992

15. Jay Shetty, www.youtube.com, *http://www.youtube.com/@jayshetty*

About the Author

Efrat holds a Bachelor's Degree in Biology from the University of Massachusetts and a Doctorate of Pharmacy from Northeastern University. Although no longer practicing as a pharmacist, she draws upon both her healthcare background and over two decades of personal experience living with PTSD.

Through this book, Efrat shares practical ideas and lessons that have helped her navigate trauma while continuing to build a meaningful and fulfilling life. Her goal is to help others feel less alone and offer supportive guidance for the challenges that trauma can bring.

Efrat spends some of free time working on her other creative endeavors, such as knitting, along with watching American Football or the National Football League (NFL) during the NFL season.

www.ingramcontent.com/pod-product-compliance
Lightning Source LLC
LaVergne TN
LVHW040521210926
848480LV00007BA/1550
* 9 7 9 8 2 3 4 2 0 3 8 3 0 *